BODY

SEX SIGNALS

Published by Ideas Unlimited (Publishing)

Ideas Unlimited (Publishing)
P.O. Box 125, Portsmouth,
Hampshire PO1 4PP

ISBN 1 871964 06 7

Cover designed by Preface Design
Printed in Great Britain.

CONTENTS

CONTENTS (CONTINUED)

INTRODUCTION

Walking through the street of a foreign land, not able to speak the language or understand the customs, one is bound to feel a little nervous. Yet people go through life, completely oblivious to the most important language in everyday use. That of **BODY LANGUAGE**.

It is a language which is being used every second of the day, usually quite unintentionally, but always accurately. Understanding it would open up new horizons, and completely change the way you observe others. Ignoring it could mean missed opportunities, and often disastrous consequences.

This book will attempt to cover the basic courtship gestures of the language, how they are misunderstood, and how one can begin to pick up phrases from everyday situations, and put them to good use.

THE PARTS OF A GIRL'S ANATOMY GUYS LIKE, AND WHAT IT REVEALS.

Hair: The colour of a girl's hair, its length and style, all reveal aspects of the image the girl would like to portray. A long blonde haired girl is seen to be sexy and playful, and a short dark haired girl may attract a more serious and sophisticated man.

Legs: Guys who consider a girl's legs as her most important asset, are usually the adventurous and unfaithful type.

Breasts: Guys who like small breasts are usually more thoughtful and intellecutal, whilst those who prefer the larger breasts are more sporty and athletic. Guys who like breasts regardless of size, think they are sporty.

Bottom: Guys who like the girls bottoms are often the mature, responsible type, as well as being a potential family man.

Face: Guys who go for the individual features of a girl's face, and the subtle expressions are usually very sensitive and gentle type.

Brain: The guys who say that the most important part of a girl's anatomy is her brain, are either very dishonest, or just crazy.

THE PARTS OF A GUY'S ANATOMY GIRLS LIKE, AND WHAT IT REVEALS.

Hair: Girls who consider a guy's hair as important are usually very romantic, and often dream about a Mills & Boon romance with an attractive man.

Muscles: Muscles signify strength and provider of security. Girls who like muscles in a man consider security as important. A fine toned man is also seen as sexually more attractive and competent.

Small Bottom: Women who like small muscular bottoms on a man are considered to have healthy sexual desires, and are often the type who undress a man with their eyes.

Hairy chest: Women who like hairy chests, are usually those who desire to be held on to and cared for. The cuddles are usually as important as what follows.

Facial hair/Stubble: Women who like stubble on a man are usually after a masculine, tough image of a hunter.

Personality: Most women would include personality to their shopping list, but often fail to give a man the chance if the above criteria are not there.

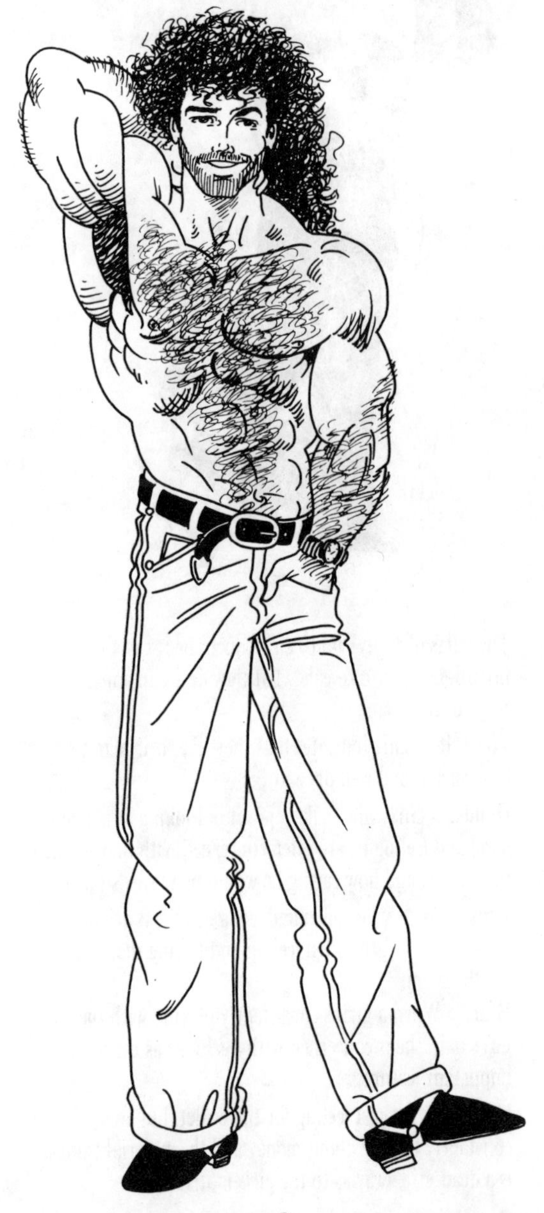

THE BITS OF A GUY GIRLS TOUCH AND WHY.

The parts of a guy's body girls touch, be it casually or intentionally, also reveals what they desire in a man. If they touch a man's. . . .

Tie: It usually indicates that they like their man to look smart, and well dressed.

Hands: Girls who make a point of looking at a man's hand and feeling it, are often concerned with how gentle the man is, and how caring he would be towards them.

Legs: Girls who touch and feel a guy's legs are on the sexual wave length, often feeling and testing the water for the swim.

Hair: When a girl is consistently playing with the guy's hair, she is concerned with his looks as the most important feature.

Money: Not just feeling for the wallet, but even constantly talking about money and the material things, is a dead give away as to the girls motives.

THE BITS OF A GIRL GUYS TOUCH AND WHY.

Men, as unlikely as it may sound, are more reserved than women when it comes to touching someone they have just met. Of all the desirable parts they wish they could touch, the hands are usually the safest form of bodily contact they finally go for.

THE GIRLS' 'COME ON' SIGNALS.

A – Standing with legs slightly apart.
B – Fondling objects such as pencils, etc.
C – Mouth slightly open with wet lips.
D – Longer than average gazes.
E – Looking with dilated pupils.
F – Gazing with tilted head.
G – Foot pointing towards the victim.

THE GIRLS' 'COME ON' SIGNALS.

H – Postruded chest and general high muscle tone.
I – Playing with or patting hair into position.
J – Head flicked back to toss hair over the shoulders.
K – Gazing with dropped eyelids.
L – Showing off the bare skin on wrists, arms, legs
M – Lips, cheeks and breasts get redder and bigger.
N – Rubbing of the arm, hands etc. against the body.

THE GUYS' 'COME ON' SIGNALS.

A – Standing with legs slightly apart.
B – Thumbs in the pocket, fingers pointing at genitals.
C – Thrusting pelvis forward.
D – Displaying preening behaviour.
E – Intimate gaze.
F – High muscle tone, accentuating physical size.
G – Feet positioned to point away from each other.

THE GUYS' 'COME ON' SIGNALS.

H – Rearranging the tie or other clothing.
I – Thrusting the chin forward.
J – Hands in the pocket, hiding the sweaty palms.
K – Controlled grin.
L – Getting red and hot around the collar.
M – Fingers pointing at genitals.
N – Slight loss of balance.

'QUIETLY INTERESTED' SIGNALS.

The 'I am interested' signals are sometimes very subtle, and could very easily be missed. The guy whilst having the preening behaviour with one hand in the pocket, is covering up his mouth with the other. This is perhaps to cover up the watering of the mouth or even the tongue hanging out. Couples with such subtle signals are usually anxious about the other persons feelings, and to avoid the risk of making a fool of themselves.

'LOOK I AM INTERESTED' SIGNALS.

On the other hand some couples tend to accentuate their 'come on' signals by putting on an exhibition. The guy is showing off his manhood, whilst the girl being very interested is trying to mirror his image. A number of courtship gestures mentioned previously are also being displayed.

THE GUYS' 'I AM IN LOVE' SIGNALS.

The guy has fallen in love, and the girl is obviously enjoying every minute of it. He has lost his cool, and to some degree the control of his bodily balance and actions. Other unmistakable signals being displayed include; the eyes popping out, tongue hanging down, and the lighting of a lit cigarette. The girl on the other hand while displaying slightly more subtle signals is also interested. She is fondling the stem of her wine glass, hip flicked to one side, legs a little apart, gazing out of the corner of her eyes.

THE GIRLS' 'I WANT YOU' SIGNALS.

Some girls on the other hand realising the guys' ignorance of body language, try not so subtle gestures. The girl above whilst stroking her neck as a sign of being HOT, legs apart with knees almost touching the other persons, is making sure the message is understood by her casual touch. The touch is sometimes portrayed as accidental, but is always an intention to invade the other persons space and get intimate.

THE GUYS' 'OOOH I AM IN LOVE' SIGNALS.

Guys seem to fall in love rather quicker than girls. Some guys have been known to fall in love as often as twenty times on one single day on the beach. The guy above realising how pathetic his actions are anyway, on seeing someone so attractive, that he is trying to prevent the girl from having anything else to laugh about by covering his most humorous assets, at the same time pointing at the part of his body responsible for his actions.

THE GIRLS' 'I AM IN LOVE' SIGNALS.

The signals sent out by a girl who has fallen in love are rather more subtle. Her stomach is pulled in, she begins to look at her feet, with a certain glow about her. Her body begins to produce a stimulant making the heart beat faster, and also produce a special mating scent. The guy even if having missed the signals has smelt trouble, and like a number of men, is running away from commitment.

THE INTERESTED GIRL AND THE INSECURE GUY.

Guys are constantly looking for the 'come on' signals from girls, and when these signals are not forthcoming, they are usually made up or imagined. The fact is that some guys would not recognise a 'come on' signal if it hit them on the head. The man above is being sent the most obvious of signals, and yet he is still seeking reassurance from his friend before making a move.

THE GIRLS' 'I WANT A SECOND OPINION ABOUT YOU' SIGNALS.

The reason why girls tend to go to the wash room more often than men, has nothing to do with their bodily biological functions. That is where meetings are held to discuss the events at ten minutes intervals. They return after discussing the suitability of the guys around, and the decision taken at the meeting is usually made quite obvious by their actions immediately following their return.

THE GUYS' 'IS THIS MY LUCKY DAY, OR WHAT?' LOOK.

The girl standing at the bar is sending out signals of availability. Her hip tossed to one side, and general preening gesture. The guy cannot believe his luck, and is approaching her like a cat crawling towards his prey, quietly, softly and cautiously, with a look which tells the whole story.

JUST MET AND HITTING IT OFF.

A couple just met and hitting it off. The guy enclosing the girls space, shutting off her escape route is demanding time to sweet talk her. His intentions are unmistakable, the cowboy pose, with fingers again pointing at his ultimate goal. The girl on the other hand is also interested. Her hand playing with her cheeks and lips. Her feet pointing straight at the guy, legs slightly apart, and playing hide and seek behind the skirt. The smile of cautious acceptance, giving the guy the benefit of the doubt.

THE GIRLS' 'YOU MUST BE JOKING' SIGNALS.

Due to most guys' reluctance to accept the girls' 'I am not interested' signals, the girls have been forced to exaggerate these signals to get the message across. The guy is obviously very interested with his cowboy pose, chin thrusted forwards, pelvis also as forward as it will go. The girl whilst securing all bodily defensive signals, still cannot believe that the guy is serious. Her folded arms, head taken back to maintain the minimum comfortable distance away.

THE GIRLS' 'I AM NOT INTERESTED' SIGNALS.

Some guys not only approach girls who are not interest, but also insist on thinking that they are interested really, and that they are just playing hard to get. Or even the reason for them throwing up could be that they have been mixing their drinks.

THE GIRLS' 'I AM REALLY NOT INTERESTED. OK?' SIGNALS.

There are times that body language is just not enough to get rid of unwanted pests. On such occasions the girl decides on a more drastic action. On these occasions, the guy usually fails to give up and insists that violence in a girl is closely associated with love . . .

THE GIRLS' 'OH NO . . . HE'S COMING OVER' LOOK.

To save loss of face, a guy should try to pick up the signals on his route towards the girl. If she tries to hide her face, and on the whole become invisible, with little peaks through her hands hiding her face. It does not mean she is playing games, but rather wishing somebody would beam her up.

FACIAL EXPRESSIONS: 'LICK MY . . . LIPS'.

This is the most commonly used facial expression. It is either signalled intentionally as shown with dropped eyelids and chin thrusted forward; or signalled by someone who would deny they meant anything by it. Either way it is a very flattering 'come on' signal. Its meaning is traditionally associated with the wet genitals, signifying the readiness for love.

FACIAL EXPRESSIONS: 'I AM TRYING TO BE SEXY'.

Guys too, try to imitate this gesture in the hope of looking as sexy as when performed by a girl. The results, however, are usually pretty disgusting. Turning out to look like they are finishing off the remains of the curry left over around the mouth from the night before.

FACIAL EXPRESSIONS: 'KISS ME YOU FOOL'.

Lips puckered up, eyes half closed, with an undeniable grin, is seen by some men as a sure signal that they have hit the jackpot. It is in fact some girls method of teasing, aimed at anyone the girl wishes to humour. Look at these sexy lips. The real thing is out of the question, this is all you'll get.

FACIAL EXPRESSIONS: 'BITE ME'.

The biting of the lips is the most erotic of the facial expressions. It is usually associated with finding someone so desirable, that they are either good enough to eat, or be eaten by. Again it is a gesture often claimed to be performed unintentionally. Either way it reveals that the girl is responding to the company, even if it means they are just being shy.

FACIAL EXPRESSIONS: 'HELLO DARLING. IT'S YOUR LUCKY DAY'.

This is a guy desperately trying to look cool. The closed mouth grin, the one raised eyebrow and the tilted head; all work together to get his message across. The message being, 'Hello darling . . . It's your lucky day'.

FACIAL EXPRESSIONS: 'I AM GOING TO BE SICK'.

This facial expression is usually prompted by seeing the last expression performed well. The eyes and eyebrows distort, the cheeks swell up, and the head projects forwards. The example shown is of course a little exaggerated; it is never-the-less, a gesture often seen on a girl's face, when approached by the less than desirable character.

FACIAL EXPRESSIONS: 'THANKS . . . BUT NO THANKS'.

This is the most misleading of all facial expressions. Whilst falling in the category of smiles, it is as false as they come. The mouth usually extending, but remaining closed. The polite smile portrays the message of 'Thanks . . . But no thanks'.

FACIAL EXPRESSIONS: 'WOW . . . SHE LIKES ME'.

The expression above is that of a guy believing that he has found the girl of his dreams, who is also very interested. The scratching of the head is of course to help him think and analyse how his luck changed so suddenly. Unfortunately for him, he may just be the recipient of a polite smile just described.

SITTING EXPRESSIONS: 'I AM NOT INTERESTED'.

The first of the sitting expressions, and it is a case of misunderstood gestures. The girl is obviously not interested; her body pointing away from the guy, arms folded, legs crossed and pointing at a clear space (the route for escape). Discreet glances watching out for any sudden approach.

The guy on the other hand, believes that she is interested really, and just playing hard to get. He is leaning towards his prey, his hands rubbing together signifying achievement in his potential.

SITTING EXPRESSIONS: 'I MAY BE INTERESTED'.

The above sitting expression portrays the guy as again on the hunt, with his legs crossed towards the girl, making sure of his intentions, but still weighing up his chances.
The girl is also quietly interested, but needs more convincing before moving closer. Her body almost pointing towards the guy, and her hands fidgeting uncontrollably. Both have made a good start, but still need convincing before making the ultimate move.

SITTING EXPRESSIONS: 'I AM VERY INTERESTED'.

The above couple are really hitting it off. She is leaning towards the guy, one arm positioned close enough to the guy for the accidental touch. Her hand holding back her hair revealing her neck. Legs slightly apart, and sitting so casually, not noticing how much leg is being exposed. The guy too, is very interested, patting his hair into position, legs as wide open as possible. His arm stretched out behind her signifying that the individual spaces have been treaded on with approval.

SITTING EXPRESSIONS: 'TOUCH ME YOU FOOL'.

This is another example of both parties interested, but sending out slightly different messages. The girl showing her interest by having her legs crossed and pointing directly at the guy, as well as fidgeting with her jewellry, her neck etc. She is also stroking her bare legs, showing off how soft they are to touch. This stroking of the legs usually signifies the girls desire to be touched. The guy is obviously so interested in what is happening, that he is on guard for the word to go further.

SITTING EXPRESSIONS: 'IGNORE HIM, HE'LL GO AWAY'.

The guy sitting on the right is kicking himself and is feeling generally annoyed at missing an opportunity by not moving fast enough. The guy in the middle having seen an empty space moved in and is now appearing to be hitting it off very nicely. Her gestures signifying her interest are; playing with her hair, toned up muscles with protruded chest. Her leg resting within the boundaries defined by the guy's legs.

SITTING EXPRESSIONS: 'TAKE ME, I AM YOURS'.

Some girls lose patience waiting for the guy to read their 'come on' signals, that they decide to take the matter in their own hands. She is obviously very interested in him, and does not waste time playing with her hair or even pointing her legs at him, she is going for the kill.
The guy whilst not believing his luck, is rather puzzled and shocked, as most guys are when the girls take the initiative.

A DESPERATE MAN'S CHAT UP LINES.

1 – Could you tell me where the bar is?
2 – Would you like a cigarette?
3 – Have you got a light?
4 – Can I buy you a drink?
5 – Have you got the time?
6 – Do you come here often?
7 – Don't I know you from somewhere?
8 – Hasn't the weather been nice?
9 – Can I offer you a lift?

A DESPERATE MAN'S PLOYS TO TOUCH A GIRL.

1 – Haven't you got big muscles?
2 – Are you ticklish?
3 – Lets have a look at your necklace.
4 – What a lovely material your dress is made of. Let's feel.
5 – Let's compare our tans.
6 – You have something stuck to your skin. Let me take it.

THE AVAILABLE GIRL AT THE DISCO 9 P.M.

9 p.m. Just arrived, she is sitting quite reserved, with very little body language. Straightened body, protruding the chest. She is hoping that her beauty is enough to attract the guys. Anyhow, there is plenty of time yet.

THE AVAILABLE GIRL AT THE DISCO 11 P.M.

11 p.m. She has decided that a few body language signals are in fact necessary to tell the guys she is available. Folded arm resting on her hip, tilted head, as well as revealing a few bits of bare skin.

THE AVAILABLE GIRL AT THE DISCO 1 A.M.

1 a.m. She is getting desperate and not so subtle with her signals. Her legs crossed open, and her arms stretched behind her head. This being the most direct invitation signal, portraying ones openness to any offers.

THE AVAILABLE GIRL AT THE DISCO 3 A.M.

3 a.m. She has waited and waited and is now totally fed up and disheartened. The smile has disappeared, and head no longer tilted, but resting in her hands. To any girl in this situation, one consolation could be that guys often shy away from attractive girls in the fear of being rejected.

THE AVAILABLE MAN AT THE PARTY (EARLY ON).

It is a fact that most guys are on constant look out for potential partners. Some are quite discreet, whilst others no matter how hard they try, end up looking very amusing. The guy above is making it quite obvious that he intends to get lucky tonight, and is open to absolutely any offers. Like a spider, he has made a web out of the sofa, and is ready to catch anything that comes near. His shirt, legs and arms wide open. This type of character is invaluable at parties. Positioning the sofa near the food, he could keep everyone so far away, that the food would last for ever.

THE AVAILABLE MAN AT THE PARTY (LATER ON).

It is only a matter of time, that he realises no one is willing to take up his offer. He therefore in an attempt to keep his pride intact, either falls asleep or pretends that he has fallen asleep, to show that he is really not interested in the company, and is only there for the grub.

THE GIRLS' 'I WANT YOU' SIGNALS.

There are of course times when the girl sends out all the right signals known to her, but in vain, as competition is pretty tough at times.
Here she is standing stroking her slim waist line, sleeves pushed back to reveal the delicate skin of her arms. Legs open, and the smile telling the whole story.

THE GIRLS' 'I WANT TO' SIGNALS.

Some girls are prepared to compete with cars, but when it comes to being ignored despite the 'come ons', for football on television, they begin to wonder.
The girl is sitting with head tossed back, playing with her lips, as well as the sexual closed eyes. She is fondling, with the stem of her wine glass, and if all that is not enough, she is also sitting absolutely naked. The guy may of course be waiting for half time.

THE GIRL IS IN LOVE, SO IS THE GUY.

The courtship signals displayed by the girl above include; standing with legs apart, thumbs in the belt with other fingers pointing at her genitals (the classic cowboy pose). Her mouth slightly open with lips looking pretty wet. High muscle tone, raised shoulders, and a long gaze with dropped eyelids.
The guy is also sending out signals of his own, but in quite a different way.

THE GIRL LIKES THE GUY, AND SO DOES THE GUY.

The above scene is some girls nightmare, and others fantasy. Nightmare for not realising the obvious, and fantasy because of its challenge. The courtship signals being sent out by the girl above include; sitting in a revealing fashion showing off the long legs, which are being rubbed together with the motion which also allows the shoe to come on and off the foot. Despite all this, she had to resort to dragging the guy by the shirt to get his attention. The guy on the other hand has also fallen in love, revealed by his signals, in particular the bent wrist.

GUYS ARE MORE DESIRABLE TO OTHERS WHEN ON A DATE.

It is unfortunate that when a guy is on his own, there is not a girl in sight who looks remotely interested. But when on a date with someone, other girls are all around sending out the signals he had only dreamt about. It is of course his unavailability which some girls find so attractive.

CLOTHES OVERKILL (TO COVER OR NOT TO COVER).

Clothes play a very important part in revealing the intended signals. Whilst it is important what parts of the body clothes on a girl reveal or hide, it does not necessarily follow that less is better. Guys often like to use their imagination, rather than being faced with the ultimate.

THE GUYS ON THE BEACH.

To some guys the beach is like a theatre, where they perform and exhibit their assets in the hope of being spotted by the person looking for their type of physique.

CHARACTER ANALYSIS ACCORDING TO HOW ONE LOOKS AT OTHERS.

The way people look at others reveals a lot about their character.

A – Accidental look: This type of look is given by people who are either very reserved to the point of not being interested, or by those just being dishonest.

B – Crafty look: This type of look is given by people who are either very shy, or they just want to tease. The girl above is looking at the guy in her mirror.

C – Obvious look: This type of look is given by fun loving, uncomplicated people, who look at what they find attractive and are very open about it to the point of being rude.

D – Invisible look: This is the type of look which is given by people whose actions, speak loud enough without the need for looking, and hence risking being caught.
The girl above is sending out enough signals through her sitting gesture and the way she is nibbling at her chocolate.

THE ALTERNATIVES TO BODY LANGUAGE.

The alternative to understanding the basics of body language, is either to carry a banner with your intentions written on it, and expect everyone else to do the same. Or just carry on blindly, until one day you make a complete ass of yourself.

OTHER TITLES AVAILABLE FROM IDEAS UNLIMITED (PUBLISHING)

OTHER TITLES AVAILABLE FROM IDEAS UNLIMITED (PUBLISHING)